Pebble Plus

Weather Basics

Snow

by Erin Edison

Consulting Editor: Gail Saunders-Smith, PhD

CAPSTONE PRESS
a capstone imprint

Pebble Plus is published by Capstone Press,
1710 Roe Crest Drive, North Mankato, Minnesota 56003.
www.capstonepub.com

Copyright © 2012 by Capstone Press, a Capstone imprint. All rights reserved.
No part of this publication may be reproduced in whole or in part, or stored in a retrieval system, or transmitted in any form or by any means, electronic, mechanical, photocopying, recording, or otherwise, without written permission of the publisher. For information regarding permission, write to Capstone Press,
1710 Roe Crest Drive, North Mankato, Minnesota 56003.

Library of Congress Cataloging-in-Publication Data
Edison, Erin.
 Snow / by Erin Edison.
   p. cm.—(Pebble plus. Weather basics)
 Summary: "Simple text and full-color photographs describe snow and how it affects people"—Provided by publisher.
 Includes bibliographical references and index.
 ISBN 978-1-4296-6059-4 (library binding)
 ISBN 978-1-4296-7080-7 (paperback)
 ISBN 978-1-4296-8755-3 (saddle-stitch)
 1. Snow—Juvenile literature. I. Title. II. Series.
QC926.37.E35 2012
551.57'84—dc22   2010054204

Editorial Credits
Erika L. Shores, editor; Kyle Grenz, designer; Laura Manthe, production specialist

Photo Credits
Alamy: Alaska Stock LLC, 17, Paul Gordon, 11; Getty Images Inc.: LOOK/Konrad Wothe, 7; PhotoEdit Inc.: Barbara Stitzer, 13; Shutterstock: Adam Gryko, back cover, Christian Lagerek, 1, Losevsky Pavel, 5, Morgan Lane Photography, 15, Steve Collender, 9, Veronika Vasilyuk, cover, Yuriy Kulyk, 21; Super Stock Inc.: Prisma, 19

Artistic Effects
Shutterstock: marcus55

Capstone Press thanks Mike Shores, earth science teacher at RBA Public Charter School in Mankato, Minnesota, for his assistance on this book.

Note to Parents and Teachers

The Weather Basics series supports national science standards related to earth science. This book describes and illustrates snow. The images support early readers in understanding the text. The repetition of words and phrases helps early readers learn new words. This book also introduces early readers to subject-specific vocabulary words, which are defined in the Glossary section. Early readers may need assistance to read some words and to use the Table of Contents, Glossary, Read More, Internet Sites, and Index sections of the book.

Table of Contents

What Is Snow?...... 4
Types of Snow 12
Snow Dangers....... 16
Melting 20

Glossary 22
Read More 23
Internet Sites 23
Index 24

What Is Snow?

Snow is frozen bits of water falling from clouds.
It is cold and soft.
It piles up on the ground.

When the air is cold, water vapor forms ice crystals in clouds. Ice crystals gather together to form snowflakes. This process is a form of condensation.

When snowflakes fall from clouds, it's called precipitation. Most snowflakes have six sides. But every snowflake is different.

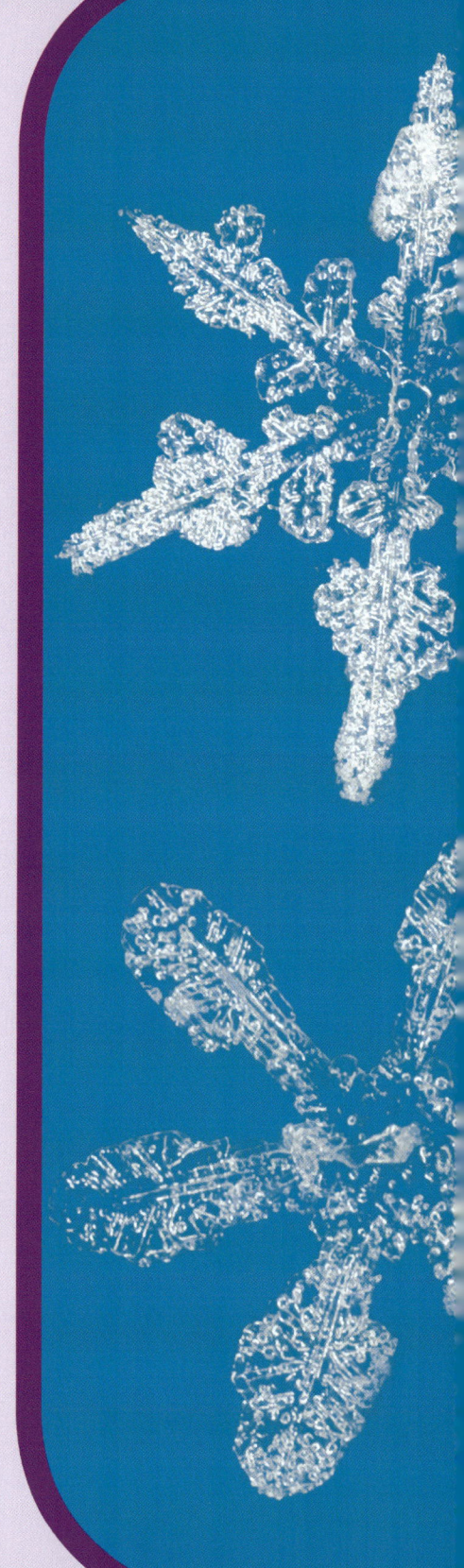

9

The air temperature must be near freezing for snowflakes to reach the ground. Temperatures above freezing turn snowflakes to rain.

Types of Snow

Some snow is soft and dry.

It feels like powder.

People sled or ski on it.

Some snow is wet.

Wet snow sticks together.

People make snowmen

and snowballs out of it.

Snow Dangers

Blizzards are windy snowstorms. People cannot see through blizzards. Snow falls quickly and blows into drifts.

Avalanches happen when huge piles of snow slide down a mountain. Avalanches bury everything in their paths.

Melting

When the weather is warm, snow melts.

It soaks into the ground.

It runs off into streams.

Snow becomes water.

Glossary

avalanche—a large mass of ice, snow, or earth that suddenly moves down the side of a mountain

blizzard—a heavy snowstorm with strong wind; a blizzard can last several days

condensation—the act of turning from a gas into a liquid

crystal—a solid made of small parts that form a pattern; snowflakes and frost are ice crystals

drift—a pile of snow caused by the wind

precipitation—water that falls from clouds to the earth's surface; precipitation can be rain, hail, sleet, or snow

water vapor—water in the form of a gas; water vapor is made of tiny bits of water that cannot be seen

Read More

Mayer, Cassie. *Snow.* Weather Watchers. Chicago: Heinemann Library, 2007.

Sterling, Kristin. *It's Snowy Today.* Lightning Bolt Book. Minneapolis: Lerner Publications Co., 2010.

Internet Sites

FactHound offers a safe, fun way to find Internet sites related to this book. All of the sites on FactHound have been researched by our staff.

Here's all you do:

Visit www.facthound.com

Type in this code: 9781429660594

Check out projects, games and lots more at www.capstonekids.com

Index

avalanches, 18
blizzards, 16
clouds, 4, 6, 8
condensation, 6
drifts, 16
ice crystals, 6
melting, 20
precipitation, 8, 10

rain, 10
skiing, 12
sledding, 12
snowballs, 14
snowflakes, 6, 8, 10
snowmen, 14
temperature, 10
water vapor, 6

Word Count: 169
Grade: 1
Early-Intervention Level: 18